SOCIAL CHANGE
LEADERSHIP INVENTORY
Self-Assessment and Analysis

Fourth Edition

CURTIS L. BRUNGARDT

Kendall Hunt
publishing company

Cover image © Shutterstock Inc.

www.kendallhunt.com
Send all inquiries to:
4050 Westmark Drive
Dubuque, IA 52004-1840

Printed in the United States of America
10 9 8 7 6 5 4 3 2

CONTENTS

INTRODUCTION

◆ Rationale

The *Social Change Leadership Inventory: Self-Assessment and Analysis* workbook is a supplement to the *Social Change Leadership (SCL) Inventory*, and is designed to assist you in learning more about your individual leadership capabilities. The *SCL Inventory* allows you to carefully evaluate your leadership potential based on the popular "social change" model of leadership development and education. The purpose of this workbook and the *SCL Inventory* is to provide you with important feedback that you can utilize to improve your ability to act as a collaborative social change agent.

◆ Understanding and Practice

The *SCL Inventory* and the *Social Change Leadership Inventory: Self-Assessment and Analysis* workbook stress the importance of both understanding the basic concepts of leadership, as well as the ability to effectively practice leadership behavior. Ultimately, successful leaders and change agents have a general knowledge of leadership, collaboration, and change and are also committed to and actually participate in collaborative change making.

◆ Reliability

The *SCL Inventory* has a strong record of both reliability and validity. First, the *SCL Inventory's* internal reliability ranges from .80 to .94. This range indicates that the questions are highly correlated within each scale. Second, the *SCL Inventory* also has high face validity. This means that the questions make sense to participants. Several focus groups reported that they were able to understand the purpose and context of the questions listed. In summary, this instrument is both reliable and valid; it measures what it intends to measure, and it accurately measures individual performance.

◆ For Best Results

In order to obtain the best feedback from the *SCL Inventory*, it is imperative that you be honest and choose the responses that most accurately describe your understanding and practice of leadership. It is also important to note that there are no right or wrong answers to the *SCL Inventory* statements. Rather, your responses should indicate your personal views and experiences in leadership.

INTRODUCTION

◆ Can I Improve My Leadership Skills?

The answer is yes. The purpose of this instrument is to provide you with immediate feedback regarding your understanding and practice of leadership. With this assessment information, you can begin the process of enhancing your leadership capabilities. The second portion of this workbook, *The Next Step: Doing Social Change Leadership*, provides you with an exercise to do just that.

WHAT IS LEADERSHIP?

Before completing the *Social Change Leadership Inventory*, take a moment to answer the following questions based on your current understanding and knowledge of leadership.

1. How do you define leadership?

_____

_____

_____

_____

_____

_____

_____

_____

2. Who do you believe is an effective leader and why?

_____

_____

_____

_____

_____

_____

_____

_____

_____

_____

WHAT IS LEADERSHIP?

3. What characteristics or traits do you believe an effective leader must have to be successful?

_____

_____

_____

_____

_____

_____

_____

_____

_____

_____

_____

4. Describe one situation in which you personally observed an effective leader. What made him or her effective and why?

_____

_____

_____

_____

_____

_____

_____

_____

_____

_____

WHAT IS LEADERSHIP?

5. Describe one situation in which you personally observed an ineffective leader. What hindered him or her from being effective?

_____

_____

_____

_____

_____

_____

_____

_____

_____

_____

_____

_____

6. What makes leadership different from traditional management?

_____

_____

_____

_____

_____

_____

_____

_____

_____

_____

_____

_____

WHAT IS LEADERSHIP?

7. **As you reflect back on your own experiences, share a situation where you served as an *effective* leader:**

_____

_____

_____

_____

_____

_____

_____

_____

_____

_____

_____

8. **As you reflect back on you own experiences, share a situation where you served as an *ineffective* leader:**

_____

_____

_____

_____

_____

_____

_____

_____

_____

_____

SOCIAL CHANGE MODEL OF LEADERSHIP

Today it seems that few of us are willing to stand up and address the serious problems facing our society. Many of us seem uninterested in making a difference in our own communities. Societal indicators show that as social problems increase, public activism decreases. This trend suggests that we need to encourage and motivate ourselves and our fellow citizens to develop skills and commit our energies to community activities that will truly benefit society.

Our goal should be to develop "social change agents" who will address and solve community problems that will have a lasting impact on America. The social change model of leadership development emphasizes collective action through collaboration for the purpose of addressing social needs and injustices. This approach to leadership development operates on the basic assumption that all of us have the ability to serve as leaders and therefore should participate in civic action for the purpose of making a difference in our communities.

While there are several theoretical frameworks that articulate the social change model of leadership development, all include three key themes: *creating change, collaboration*, and *civic leadership*. Conceptually defined, leadership is about *creating change*. Consistent with contemporary definitions, leadership is about making both personal and organizational changes. *Collaborative leadership* tells us we need new approaches to how we practice and participate in the leadership process. Finally, the *civic leadership* focus provides the meaning and a sense of purpose for our leadership involvement.

◆ Creating Change

First and foremost, leadership is about creating change. The very concept of change is what makes leadership different from all other forms of human interaction. Leadership is a process of change where both leaders and followers alike serve as change agents. Thus, those actively involved in leadership are not merely the subjects of change, but rather, the driving force behind that change. They are responsible for moving the team, organization, or community from "what is" to "what ought to be."

There are several other important elements to the creating change theme. First, leadership is about "purposefully" seeking change. More than just natural or obvious change, it is change making that is intentionally designed and implemented by the change agents. Second, leadership involves transformational or fundamental change, rather than small incremental adjustments. In most cases, it is change that requires long-term commitment. Third, the purpose of change is positive movement. Therefore, leadership is about making improvements and correcting discrepancies between "what is" and "what ought to be" for all.

♦ Collaboration

If leadership is creating and encouraging useful change, then the next question is how to initiate and sustain those changes. The answer is collaboration. It is critically important that our methods of practicing leadership reflect a more contemporary view of organizational life if we hope to be successful. These approaches are characterized by cooperation, power-sharing, and empowerment. Today teams, organizations, and communities that are successful are those who bring people together for collective action.

♦ Civic Leadership

The third and final theme focuses on why we should practice and participate in leadership. If leadership is an influence relationship for change, and collaborative approaches are the preferred methods, then the final step in the process is to encourage change that will result in improvements for society. We need to ask ourselves and others to believe in something larger than personal self-interest as we become active players in the leadership process. The civic theme represents a shift from leadership that emphasizes goal attainment for the collective good (the good of groups or organizations) to leadership that emphasizes the common good (the good of society as a whole). This theme encourages all of us to take action on behalf of this larger good. Very simply, each citizen has a responsibility to carry change forward.

SOCIAL CHANGE LEADERSHIP QUESTIONS

1. Describe the characteristics of an successful organizational leader:

_____

_____

_____

_____

_____

_____

_____

_____

_____

_____

_____

_____

_____

2. Describe the characteristics of a successful social change leader:

_____

_____

_____

_____

_____

_____

_____

_____

_____

_____

_____

SOCIAL CHANGE LEADERSHIP QUESTIONS

3. In your opinion, what is the difference between the average person and a very active citizen?

_____

_____

_____

_____

_____

_____

_____

_____

_____

_____

_____

_____

4. What do you believe it will take to motivate you to become an active social change leader?

_____

_____

_____

_____

_____

_____

_____

_____

_____

_____

EXPLAINING THE SCL INVENTORY

The *Social Change Leadership (SCL) Inventory* is a self-reporting assessment instrument designed to measure both your understanding and practice of leadership. The *SCL Inventory* allows you to carefully evaluate your leadership potential based on the "social change" approach to leadership development and education.

The first 15 statements (1 - 15) assess your basic knowledge and understanding of leadership, collaboration, and social change. Record your responses by drawing a circle around the number that best indicates your level of agreement. You have five choices:

1	2	3	4	5
No	Little	Some	Good	Substantial
Knowledge	Knowledge	Knowledge	Knowledge	Knowledge

The second 15 statements (16 - 30) assess the extent to which you actually engage in leadership behavior, collaboration, and social change. Record your responses by drawing a circle around the number that best corresponds with your practice of leadership. You have five choices:

1	2	3	4	5
	Once In		Fairly	Almost
Rarely	A While	Sometimes	Often	Always

After completing the *SCL Inventory*, please transfer your responses to page 16 of this workbook. Then follow instructions for scoring and interpretation.

Now take a few minutes and complete the *Social Change Leadership Inventory* on pages 59–64. Then transfer your responses from the survey to pages 16 and 17 of this workbook. It is not necessary to complete the last page of the survey when using this book.

SCORING YOUR SCL INVENTORY

Your *SCL Inventory* can be scored in three different ways: first, your knowledge and understanding of leadership; second, your commitment and ability to participate in leadership; and third, your total score, which reflects both your leadership understanding and behavior.

◆ My Understanding of Leadership Score

Count the number of responses from each vertical column for **statements 1 - 15** on your *SCL Inventory*. Then multiply your response numbers by the value of that selection (as listed below). Finally, add across the values in each box for your "Understanding of Leadership" score. See Appendix page 48 for sample score sheet. Transfer this score to the appropriate box on page 17.

Number of 1 responses	Number of 2 responses	Number of 3 responses	Number of 4 responses	Number of 5 responses
x 1	x 2	x 3	x 4	x 5

◆ My Practice of Leadership Behavior Score

Now count the number of responses from each vertical column for **statements 16 - 30** on your *SCL Inventory*. Again, multiply your response numbers by the value of that selection (as listed below). Finally, add across the values in each box for your "Practice of Leadership Behavior" score. See Appendix page 48. Transfer this score to the appropriate box on page 17.

Number of 1 responses	Number of 2 responses	Number of 3 responses	Number of 4 responses	Number of 5 responses
x 1	x 2	x 3	x 4	x 5

See Appendix page 48 for sample score sheet.

SCORING YOUR SCL INVENTORY

The higher your score, the better you understand and participate in the basic principles of social change leadership.

♦ **My Understanding of Leadership**

Transfer your "Understanding of Leadership" score from page 16 . . .

> ♦ A low score ranges from 15 - 35.
> ♦ A medium score ranges from 36 - 55.
> ♦ A high score ranges from 56 - 75.

This score reflects your general knowledge and understanding of leadership.

♦ **My Practice of Leadership Behavior**

Transfer your "Practice of Leadership Behavior" score from page 16 .

> ♦ A low score ranges from 15 - 35.
> ♦ A medium score ranges from 36 - 55.
> ♦ A high score ranges from 56 - 75.

This score reflects the extent to which you actually engage in leadership behavior.

♦ **Total Score: My Understanding and Practice of Leadership**

Add your understanding and behavior subscores together
for your *SCL Inventory* total score . . . .

+

> ♦ A low score ranges from 30 - 70.
> ♦ A medium score ranges from 71 - 110.
> ♦ A high score ranges from 111 - 150.

This score reflects both your general knowledge of leadership and your commitment and participation level in social change leadership.

See Appendix page 49 for sample score sheet.

CREATING CHANGE

◆ Understanding Leadership and Change

The following inventory statements are designed to assess your basic knowledge and understanding of leadership and the change process:

1. I recognize the importance leadership plays in groups, organizations, communities, and society.
4. I am able to recognize, identify, and explain the key concepts, components, and elements of the leadership process.
7. I recognize the key roles of "change, collaboration, and civic responsibility" in the leadership process.
10. I am familiar with the concept of "change" and how it is essential to the leadership process.
13. I understand that the change process involves challenging the status quo, creating a new vision, and sustaining movement.

◆ Commitment and Participation in Change Making

The following inventory statements are designed to assess both your degree of commitment as well as your participation level as a social change agent:

16. Either as a leader or follower participating in leadership, I am committed to making positive change.
19. I actively challenge the way things are done in the groups and organizations in which I participate.
22. I actively encourage, promote, and support positive change in the groups and organizations in which I participate.
25. I work hard to sustain long-term positive change in the groups and organizations in which I participate.
28. I see myself as a "change agent" in the groups and organizations in which I participate.

CREATING CHANGE

This page provides you with two grids for recording your *creating change* scores. First, transfer your individual responses from statements 1, 4, 7, 10, and 13 to the table below. Then add these response numbers for your subtotal. See Appendix page 50 for a sample. This score reflects your knowledge and understanding of leadership and change. Transfer this subtotal to the chart on the next page under the "Understanding" section for interpretation.

Understanding Leadership and Change

	RESPONSE
1. Leadership importance	
4. Key components of the leadership process	
7. Change, collaboration, and civic responsibility	
10. Concept of change and leadership	
13. Challenging status quo, new vision, and sustaining movement	
SUBTOTAL	

Second, transfer your individual responses from statements 16, 19, 22, 25, and 28 to the table below. Then add these response numbers for your subtotal. See Appendix page 50 for sample. This score reflects your commitment and participation in change making. Transfer this subtotal to the chart on the next page under the "Participation" section for interpretation.

Commitment and Participation in Change Making

	RESPONSE
16. Committed to positive change	
19. Challenging the way things are done	
22. Encourage, promote, and support positive change	
25. Sustain long-term positive change	
28. I see myself as "change agent"	
SUBTOTAL	

Finally, add both subtotals for your *creating change* total. Again, transfer this score to the chart on the next page under the "TOTAL" section for interpretation.

See Appendix page 50 for sample score sheet.

	Creating Change			Collaboration	Civic Leadership
	Understanding	Practice	TOTAL		
H	25	25	50		
I	24	24	48		
G	23	23	46		
H	22	22	44		
	21	21	42		
	20	20	40		
	19	19	38		
M	18	18	36		
E	17	17	34		
D	16	16	32		
I	15	15	30		
U	14	14	28		
M	13	13	26		
	12	12	24		
L	11	11	22		
O	10	10	20		
W	9	9	18		
	8	8	16		
	7	7	14		
	6	6	12		
	5	5	10		

*Locate and circle your scores under the appropriate sections. Are your scores high, medium, or low?
See Appendix page 51 for a sample table.

CREATING CHANGE

Based on your *creating change* scores (pages 19 and 20), what do you believe are your **areas of strength**?

_____

_____

_____

_____

_____

_____

_____

_____

_____

_____

Based on your *creating change* scores, what do you believe are your **greatest needs for improvement**?

_____

_____

_____

_____

_____

_____

_____

_____

_____

_____

See Appendix page 52 for sample.

COLLABORATION

◆ Understanding Collaboration

The following inventory statements are designed to assess your basic knowledge and understanding of collaboration:

2. I recognize that both leaders and followers serve as partners in the leadership and change process.

5. I understand and recognize the role both personal and collaborative skills play in leadership and the change process.

8. I am able to distinguish between the group stages that lead to coordination, cooperation, and collaboration.

11. I recognize the advantages of working in groups and teams to accomplish tasks.

14. I understand that the goal of collaborative leadership is to assist people in working together to solve problems.

◆ Commitment and Participation in Collaboration

The following inventory statements are designed to assess both your degree of commitment as well as your participation level in the collaborative leadership process:

17. I demonstrate collaborative leadership skills, including the ability to successfully communicate and work with others in group settings.

20. I encourage people to work together and collaborate with one another in a team approach.

23. I treat other team members with dignity and respect.

26. I encourage team members to feel a sense of ownership for the common goals we pursue.

29. I encourage and support a climate of mutual trust among team members.

COLLABORATION

This page provides you with two grids for recording your *collaboration* scores. First, transfer your individual responses from statements 2, 5, 8, 11, and 14 to the table below. Then add these response numbers for your subtotal. This score reflects your knowledge and understanding of collaborative leadership. Transfer this subtotal to the chart on the next page under the "Understanding" section for interpretation.

Understanding Collaboration

	RESPONSE
2. Leadership and followers as partners	
5. Role of personal and collaborative skills in process	
8. Distinguish between group processes	
11. Collaborative methods offer advantages	
14. Working together to solve problems	
SUBTOTAL	

Second, transfer your individual responses from statements 17, 20, 23, 26, and 29 to the table below. Then add these response numbers for your subtotal. This score reflects your commitment and participation in collaboration. Transfer this subtotal to the chart on the next page under the "Participation" section for interpretation.

Commitment and Participation in Collaboration

	RESPONSE
17. Demonstrate collaborative leadership skills	
20. Encourage people to work together in team approach	
23. Treat team members with dignity and respect	
26. Encourage team members to feel a sense of ownership	
29. Encourage a climate of mutual trust	
SUBTOTAL	

Finally, add both subtotals for your ***collaboration* total**. Again, transfer this score to the chart on the next page under the "TOTAL" section for interpretation.

Creating Change   Collaboration   Civic Leadership

	Understanding	Practice	TOTAL
HIGH	25	25	50
	24	24	48
	23	23	46
	22	22	44
	21	21	42
	20	20	40
	19	19	38
MEDIUM	18	18	36
	17	17	34
	16	16	32
	15	15	30
	14	14	28
	13	13	26
	12	12	24
LOW	11	11	22
	10	10	20
	9	9	18
	8	8	16
	7	7	14
	6	6	12
	5	5	10

*Locate and circle your scores under the appropriate sections. Are your scores high, medium, or low?

COLLABORATION

Based on your *collaboration* scores (pages 23 and 24), what do you believe are your **areas of strength**?

_____

_____

_____

_____

_____

_____

_____

_____

_____

_____

_____

Based on your *collaboration* scores, what do you believe are your **greatest needs for improvement**?

_____

_____

_____

_____

_____

_____

_____

_____

_____

_____

CIVIC LEADERSHIP

◆ Understanding Civic Leadership

The following inventory statements are designed to assess your basic knowledge and understanding of the civic leadership philosophy:

3. I understand the relationship between leadership and citizenship.
6. I am familiar with the concept of "civic leadership" and the pursuit of change for the common (societal) good.
9. I recognize that every citizen has the ability and obligation to lead.
12. I understand that the primary role of the citizen leader is to address and solve community problems.
15. I understand that those who participate in civic leadership serve as agents of change to make our world a better place.

◆ Commitment and Participation in Civic Leadership

The following inventory statements are designed to assess both your degree of commitment as well as your participation level in civic action and leadership:

18. I serve as a citizen leader in my community.
21. I am personally committed to leadership and civic change as a way to serve others.
24. I volunteer time to serve others in the community.
27. I attend and actively participate in community meetings and forums in order to make a difference.
30. I serve as an agent of change for the purpose of making my community and world a better place.

CIVIC LEADERSHIP

This page provides you with two grids for recording your *civic leadership* scores. First, transfer your individual responses from statements 3, 6, 9, 12, and 15 to the table below. Then add these response numbers for your subtotal. This score reflects your knowledge and understanding of civic leadership. Transfer this subtotal to the chart on the next page under the "Understanding" section for interpretation.

Understanding Civic Leadership

	RESPONSE
3. Relationship between leadership and citizenship	
6. "Civic leadership" and the pursuit for common good	
9. Every citizen has the ability and obligation to lead	
12. Citizen leaders address community problems	
15. Agents of change and their involvement in civic leadership	
SUBTOTAL	

Second, transfer your individual responses from statements 18, 21, 24, 27, and 30 to the table below. Then add these response numbers for your subtotal. This score reflects your commitment and participation in civic leadership. Transfer this subtotal to the chart on the next page under the "Participation" section for interpretation.

Commitment and Participation in Civic Leadership

	RESPONSE
18. I serve as a citizen leader	
21. Personally committed to leadership and change	
24. Volunteer time and serve others in my community	
27. Attend and participate in community meetings and forums	
30. Serve as change agent for purpose of making the world better	
SUBTOTAL	

Finally, add both subtotals for your *civic leadership* total. Again, transfer this score to the chart on the next page under the "TOTAL" section for interpretation.

Creating Change | Collaboration | Civic Leadership

		Understanding	Practice	TOTAL
HIGH		25	25	50
		24	24	48
		23	23	46
		22	22	44
		21	21	42
		20	20	40
		19	19	38
MEDIUM		18	18	36
		17	17	34
		16	16	32
		15	15	30
		14	14	28
		13	13	26
		12	12	24
LOW		11	11	22
		10	10	20
		9	9	18
		8	8	16
		7	7	14
		6	6	12
		5	5	10

*Locate and circle your scores under the appropriate sections. Are your scores high, medium, or low?

CIVIC LEADERSHIP

Based on your *civic leadership* scores (pages 27 and 28), what do you believe are your **areas of strength**?

_____

_____

_____

_____

_____

_____

_____

_____

_____

Based on your *civic leadership* scores, what do you believe are your **greatest needs for improvement**?

_____

_____

_____

_____

_____

_____

_____

_____

_____

SUMMARY QUESTIONS

By transferring your change, collaboration, and civic leadership average scores to the following page, you will get a comprehensive illustration of your leadership strengths and weaknesses. First, turn back to page 20 and transfer your *creating change* scores (Understand, Practice, and TOTAL) by circling the corresponding numbers on page 31. Second, turn to page 24 and transfer your *collaboration* scores (Understanding, Practice, and TOTAL) by circling the corresponding numbers on page 31. Then, third, turn to page 28 and transfer your *civic leadership* scores (Understanding, Practice, and TOTAL) by circling the corresponding numbers on page 31.

After transferring your scores, connect your "Understanding" scores for change, collaboration, and civic leadership using a dotted line. Next, connect your "Practice" scores for change, collaboration, and civic leadership using a dashed line. Last, connect your "TOTAL" scores for change, collaboration, and civic leadership using a solid line. (See Appendix page 53 for sample.)

Now, you have the opportunity to take a comprehensive look at your abilities on all three scales of the social change leadership model. When viewing all three scales (*creating change*, *collaboration*, and *civic leadership*), what is your strongest component of the social change leadership model (your highest TOTAL score)?

_____

When viewing all three scales (*creating change*, *collaboration*, and *civic leadership*), what is the component of the social change leadership model that indicates your greatest need for improvement (your lowest TOTAL score)?

_____

What other observations can you make?

_____

_____

_____

	Creating Change			Collaboration			Civic Leadership		
	Understanding	Practice	TOTAL	Understanding	Practice	TOTAL	Understanding	Practice	TOTAL
H	25	25	50	25	25	50	25	25	50
I	24	24	48	24	24	48	24	24	48
G	23	23	46	23	23	46	23	23	46
H	22	22	44	22	22	44	22	22	44
	21	21	42	21	21	42	21	21	42
	20	20	40	20	20	40	20	20	40
	19	19	38	19	19	38	19	19	38
M	18	18	36	18	18	36	18	18	36
E	17	17	34	17	17	34	17	17	34
D	16	16	32	16	16	32	16	16	32
I	15	15	30	15	15	30	15	15	30
U	14	14	28	14	14	28	14	14	28
M	13	13	26	13	13	26	13	13	26
	12	12	24	12	12	24	12	12	24
L	11	11	22	11	11	22	11	11	22
O	10	10	20	10	10	20	10	10	20
W	9	9	18	9	9	18	9	9	18
	8	8	16	8	8	16	8	8	16
	7	7	14	7	7	14	7	7	14
	6	6	12	6	6	12	6	6	12
	5	5	10	5	5	10	5	5	10

See Appendix page 53 for a sample table.

31

SUMMARY QUESTIONS

In your own words, summarize your "Understanding" and "Practice" leadership subscores and your total leadership score from pages 16, 17, and 31. What does this feedback say about your leadership knowledge and behavior?

_____

_____

_____

_____

_____

_____

_____

_____

_____

_____

Summarize your *creating change* scores from pages 18 - 21. What does this feedback say about both your understanding of leadership and change and your commitment and participation in change making?

_____

_____

_____

_____

_____

_____

_____

_____

_____

_____

SUMMARY QUESTIONS

Summarize your *collaboration* scores from pages 22 - 25. What does this feed-back say about both your understanding of collaboration and your commitment and participation in collaborative leadership?

_____

_____

_____

_____

_____

_____

_____

_____

_____

_____

Summarize your *civic leadership* scores from pages 26 - 29. What does this feedback say about both your understanding of civic leadership and your com-mitment and participation in civic leadership?

_____

_____

_____

_____

_____

_____

_____

_____

_____

_____

The Next Step: Doing Social Change Leadership

DOING SOCIAL CHANGE LEADERSHIP

Now that you have measured your understanding, commitment, and participation in social change leadership, it is time to apply these concepts to a real community issue. Discovering your strengths and weaknesses (as illustrated by the *SCL Inventory*) is only the first step; effective citizen leaders must then put their knowledge and commitment into action.

The following seven pages of this handbook are designed to assist and guide you in your efforts to become a more active and successful citizen leader. This exercise is intended to encourage you to participate in a real community project for the purpose of improving and building upon your leadership capabilities.

Community Issue Outline:

♦ Identify Important Community Issues

♦ Select Your Community Project

♦ Develop an Overall Vision Statement

♦ Develop Action Steps and Strategies for Involvement

♦ Determine Your Role in the Community Project

♦ Potential Obstacles and Solutions

♦ Expected Results

♦ Post-Project Personal Assessment

DOING SOCIAL CHANGE LEADERSHIP

◆ **Identify Important Community Issues**

List five important problems or issues within your community that need to be addressed and changed.

1.

2.

3.

4.

5.

◆ **Select Your Community Project**

Using your list above, identify the one project in which you want to become (more) involved:

_____

Why is this issue important to you and your community?

_____
_____
_____
_____
_____
_____
_____
_____
_____
_____
_____

_____

DOING SOCIAL CHANGE LEADERSHIP

◆ Develop an Overall Vision Statement

The purpose of the vision statement is to provide you and your community group with an overall direction. Describe the ideal situation in your community, after the problem or issue has been solved or accomplished. Within this statement, include a description of specific results that your group would like to achieve. (Do not describe how it will be done, but rather, what the result will be.)

_____

_____

_____

_____

_____

_____

_____

_____

_____

_____

_____

_____

_____

_____

_____

_____

DOING SOCIAL CHANGE LEADERSHIP

♦ **Action Steps and Strategies**

Now that you have developed a vision statement for your community project, it is time to develop specific plans of action in order to reach your goal. Below is a table to assist you in your planning process.

Name of your community project:_____

ACTION STEPS AND STRATEGIES	
"What needs to be done?"	
	How: When: My Role:
	How: When: My Role:
	How: When: My Role:
	How: When: My Role:
	How: When: My Role:
	How: When: My Role:

DOING SOCIAL CHANGE LEADERSHIP

◆ Obstacles

After developing specific plans of action for the implementation of your community project, evaluate the possible obstacles you may encounter. Using the table below, list possible obstacles on the left-hand side, and in the right column list the strategies that you will use to overcome these obstacles. Remember to think of more than one possible solution for each obstacle.

Name of your community project:_____

Obstacles	Strategies to Overcome Obstacles

◆ Expected Results

If this community project is successful, what will you (or your community group) have accomplished in six months?

_____

_____

_____

_____

_____

_____

_____

_____

_____

_____

_____

_____

_____

_____

_____

_____

_____

_____

_____

_____

_____

DOING SOCIAL CHANGE LEADERSHIP

If this community project is successful, what will you (or your community group) have accomplished in one year?

_____

_____

_____

_____

_____

_____

_____

_____

_____

_____

_____

_____

_____

_____

_____

_____

_____

_____

_____

_____

_____

_____

_____

_____

_____

DOING SOCIAL CHANGE LEADERSHIP

◆ Post-Project Personal Assessment

After participating in your chosen community project, take the time to assess whether your understanding and behavior regarding change, collaboration, and civic leadership have improved. If so, how, and to what extent.

_____

_____

_____

_____

_____

_____

_____

_____

_____

_____

_____

_____

_____

_____

_____

_____

_____

_____

_____

_____

_____

_____

_____

NOTES

NOTES

NOTES

◆ APPENDIX ◆

APPENDIX

Your *SCL Inventory* can be scored in three different ways: first, your knowledge and understanding of leadership; second, your commitment and ability to participate in leadership; and third, your total score, which reflects both your leadership understanding and behavior.

◆ My Understanding of Leadership Score

Count the number of responses from each vertical column for **statements 1 - 15** on your *SCL Inventory*. Then multiply your response numbers by the value of that selection (as listed below). Finally, add across the values in each box for your "Understanding of Leadership" score. See Appendix page 49 for sample score sheet. Transfer this score to the appropriate box on page 17.

Number of 1 responses	Number of 2 responses	Number of 3 responses	Number of 4 responses	Number of 5 responses
0	8	3	2	0
x 1	x 2	x 3	x 4	x 5

$$0 + 16 + 9 + 8 + 0 = 33$$

◆ My Practice of Leadership Behavior Score

Now count the number of responses from each vertical column for **statements 16 - 30** on your *SCL Inventory*. Again, multiply your response numbers by the value of that selection (as listed below). Finally, add across the values in each box for your "Practice of Leadership Behavior" score. See Appendix page 49. Transfer this score to the appropriate box on page 17.

Number of 1 responses	Number of 2 responses	Number of 3 responses	Number of 4 responses	Number of 5 responses
0	3	4	6	2
x 1	x 2	x 3	x 4	x 5

$$0 + 6 + 12 + 24 + 10 = 52$$

APPENDIX

> *The higher your score, the better you understand and participate in the basic principles of social change leadership.*

♦ **My Understanding of Leadership**

Transfer your "Understanding of Leadership" score from page 16 . . .

33

- ♦ A low score ranges from 15 - 35.
- ♦ A medium score ranges from 36 - 55.
- ♦ A high score ranges from 56 - 75.

This score reflects your general knowledge and understanding of leadership.

♦ **My Practice of Leadership Behavior**

Transfer your "Practice of Leadership Behavior" score from page 16 .

52

- ♦ A low score ranges from 15 - 35.
- ♦ A medium score ranges from 36 - 55.
- ♦ A high score ranges from 56 - 75.

This score reflects the extent to which you actually engage in leadership behavior.

♦ **Total Score: My Understanding And Practice of Leadership**

Add your understanding and behavior subscores together for your *SCL Inventory* total score . . . .

+

85

- ♦ A low score ranges from 30 - 70.
- ♦ A medium score ranges from 71 - 110.
- ♦ A high score ranges from 111 - 150.

This score reflects both your general knowledge of leadership and your commitment and participation level in social change leadership.

This page provides you with two grids for recording your *creating change* scores. First, transfer your individual responses from statements 1, 4, 7, 10, and 13 to the table below. Then add these response numbers for your subtotal. See Appendix page 48 for a sample. This score reflects your knowledge and understanding of leadership and change. Transfer this subtotal to the chart on the next page under the "Understanding" section for interpretation.

Understanding Leadership and Change

	RESPONSE
1. Leadership importance	4
4. Key components of the leadership process	3
7. Change, collaboration, and civic responsibility	3
10. Concept of change and leadership	4
13. Challenging status quo, new vision, and sustaining movement	3
SUBTOTAL	17

Second, transfer your individual responses from statements 16, 19, 22, 25, and 28 to the table below. Then add these response numbers for your subtotal. See Appendix page 48 for sample. This score reflects your commitment and participation in change making. Transfer this subtotal to the chart on the next page under the "Participation" section for interpretation.

Commitment and Participation in Change Making

	RESPONSE
16. Committed to positive change	4
19. Challenging the way things are done	4
22. Encourage, promote, and support positive change	4
25. Sustain long-term positive change	5
28. I see myself as a "change agent"	4
SUBTOTAL	21

Finally, add both subtotals for your *creating change* total. Again, transfer this score to the chart on the next page under the "TOTAL" section for interpretation.

38

Creating Change   **Collaboration**   **Civic Leadership**

	Understanding	Practice	TOTAL	Collaboration	Civic Leadership
HIGH	25	25	50		
	24	24	48		
	23	23	46		
	22	22	44		
	21	(21)	42		
	20	20	40		
	19	19	(38)		
MEDIUM	18	18	36		
	(17)	17	34		
	16	16	32		
	15	15	30		
	14	14	28		
	13	13	26		
	12	12	24		
LOW	11	11	22		
	10	10	20		
	9	9	18		
	8	8	16		
	7	7	14		
	6	6	12		
	5	5	10		

*Locate and circle your scores under the appropriate sections. Are your scores high, medium, or low?

APPENDIX

Based on your *creating change* scores (pages 19 and 20), what do you believe are your **areas of strength**?

My highest score in the "creating change" component of the SCL Inventory was my ability to "practice" leadership and change. I had a score of 21 out of a possible 25 points which placed me in the "high" category.

Based on your *creating change* scores, what do you believe are your **greatest needs for improvement**?

My lowest score in the "creating change" component of the SCL Inventory was my "understanding" or knowledge of leadership and change. My score was 17 out of a possible 25 points which placed me in the "medium" category. This seems to suggest that my greatest need for improvement is to become more knowledgeable in the field of leadership.

	Creating Change			Collaboration			Civic Leadership		
	Understanding	Practice	TOTAL	Understanding	Practice	TOTAL	Understanding	Practice	TOTAL
HIGH	25	25	50	25	25	50	25	25	50
	24	24	48	24	24	48	24	24	48
	23	23	46	23	23	46	23	23	46
	22	22	44	22	22	44	22	22	44
	21	(21)	42	21	21	42	21	21	42
	20	20	40	20	20	40	20	20	40
	19	19	(38)	19	(19)	38	19	19	38
MEDIUM	18	18	36	18	18	36	18	18	36
	(17)	17	34	17	17	34	17	17	34
	16	16	32	16	16	(32)	16	16	32
	15	15	30	15	15	30	15	15	30
	14	14	28	(14)	14	28	14	14	28
	13	13	26	13	13	26	13	13	26
	12	12	24	12	12	24	(12)	(12)	(24)
LOW	11	11	22	11	11	22	11	11	22
	10	10	20	10	10	20	10	10	20
	9	9	18	9	9	18	9	9	18
	8	8	16	8	8	16	8	8	16
	7	7	14	7	7	14	7	7	14
	6	6	12	6	6	12	6	6	12
	5	5	10	5	5	10	5	5	10

SELECTED READINGS

A social change model of leadership development: Guidebook version III. (1996). University of California, Los Angeles: Higher Education Research Institute.

Block, P. (1993). *Stewardship: Choosing service over self-interest.* San Francisco: Berrett-Koehler.

Beaumont, Elizabeth, Jason Stephens, Thomas Ehrlich, and Anne Colby. (2003). *Educating citizens: Preparing America's undergraduates for lives of moral and civic responsibility.* San Francisco: Jossey-Bass.

Boyte, H.C. (1989). *Commonwealth: A return to citizen politics.* New York: Free Press.

Boyte, Harry C. (2008). *The citizen solution: How you can make a difference.* Saint Paul: Minnesota Historical Society.

Bryson, J.M., and B.C. Crosby (1992). *Leadership for the common good.* San Francisco: Jossey-Bass.

Chaleff, I. (1995). *The courageous follower: Standing up to and for our leaders.* San Francisco: Berrett-Koehler.

Chrislip, D.D., and D.E. Larson (1994). *Collaborative leadership: How citizens and civic leaders can make a difference.* San Francisco: Jossey-Bass.

Clawson, James G. (2009). *Level three leadership: Getting below the surface.* 4th ed. Upper Saddle River: Pearson Education.

Colby, Anne, Elizabeth Beaumont, Thomas Ehrlich, and Josh Corngold. (2007). *Educating for democracy: Preparing undergraduates for responsible political engagement.* San Francisco: Jossey-Bass.

Drath, W.H., and C.J. Palus (1994). *Making common sense: Leadership as meaning-making in a community of practice.* Greensboro, NC: Center for Creative Leadership.

SELECTED READINGS

Gardner, John W., and Francesca Gardner. (2003). *Living, leading, and the American dream.* San Francisco: Jossey-Bass.

Gardner, John W. (1990). *On leadership.* New York: The Free Press.

Hackman, J.R. (Ed.). (1990). *Groups that work (and those that don't): Creating conditions for effective teamwork.* San Francisco: Jossey-Bass.

Hannum, Kelly, Jennifer Martineau, and Claire Reinelt. (2007). *The handbook of leadership development evaluation.* San Francisco: Jossey-Bass.

Illsley, P.J. (1990). *Enhancing the volunteer experience: New insights on strengthening volunteer participation, learning, and commitment.* San Francisco: Jossey-Bass.

Jansson, Bruce S. (2003). *Becoming an effective policy advocate: From policy practice to social justice.* 4th ed. Belmont, CA: Brooks/Cole.

Kahn, S. (1991). *Organizing: A guide for the grassroots leaders.* (Rev. ed.) Silver Spring, MD: NASW Press.

Kelley, R.E. (1992). *The power of followership: How to create leaders people want to follow and followers who lead themselves.* New York: Currency/ Doubleday.

Langseth, Mark Norman., William Marmaduke Plater, and Scott Dillon. (2004). *Public work and the academy: An academic administrator's guide to civic engagement and service-learning.* Bolton, MA.: Anker Publishers.

Lumsden, G., and D. Lumsden (1993). *Communicating in groups and teams: Sharing leadership.* Belmont, CA: Wadsworth.

Northouse, Peter Guy. (2007). *Leadership: Theory and practice.* 4th ed. Thousand Oaks: Sage Publications.

O'Toole, J. (1996). *Leading change: Overcoming the ideology of comfort and the tyranny of custom.* San Francisco: Jossey-Bass.

Quinn, Robert E. (1996). *Deep change: Discovering the leader within*. San Francisco: Jossey-Bass.

Rost, Joseph C. (1993). *Leadership for the twenty-first century*. Westport, CT: Praeger Publishers.

Ruscio, Kenneth Patrick. (2008). *The leadership dilemma in modern democracy*. Cheltenham, UK: Edward Elgar.

Vago, Steven. (2004). *Social change*. 5th ed. Upper Saddle River, NJ: Pearson Prentice Hall.

Wren, J. Thomas. (1995). *The leader's companion: Insights on leadership through the ages*. New York: The Free Press.

◆ SOCIAL CHANGE LEADERSHIP INVENTORY ◆

SOCIAL CHANGE LEADERSHIP INVENTORY (4th Edition)

The *Social Change Leadership (SCL) Inventory (4th)* is a self-reporting assessment instrument designed to measure both your understanding and practice of leadership. The *SCL Inventory* allows you to carefully evaluate your leadership potential based on the popular "social change" approach to leadership development and education.

The first 15 statements (1–15) assess your basic knowledge and understanding of leadership, collaboration, and social change. Record your responses by drawing a circle around the number that best indicates your level of agreement. You have five choices:

1	2	3	4	5
No Knowledge	Little Knowledge	Some Knowledge	Good Knowledge	Substantial Knowledge

The second 15 statements (16–30) assess the extent to which you actually engage in leadership behavior, collaboration, and social change. Record your response by drawing a circle around the number that best corresponds with your practice of leadership. You have five choices:

1	2	3	4	5
Rarely	Once In A While	Sometimes	Fairly Often	Almost Always

After completing the *SCL Inventory,* please transfer your responses to the back page. Then follow instructions for scoring and interpretation.

The Social Change Model of Leadership

The social change model of leadership is based on three organizing themes: creating change, collaboration, and civic leadership. Leadership is about making personal and organizational change. Collaboration provides us with the methods for leadership participation. The civic leadership focus provides the meaning and purpose for leadership behavior.

Creating Change. First and foremost, leadership is about creating change. Leadership is a process of change where both leaders and followers alike serve as change agents. Thus, those involved are not just subjects of change, but rather the driving force for change. They are responsible for moving the team, organization, or community from "what is" to what "ought to be."

Collaboration. If leadership is creating and encouraging useful change, then the next question is "how" to initiate and sustain those changes. The answer is collaboration. It is important that leadership methods reflect our changing society, which is characterized by cooperation, power-sharing, and empowerment.

Civic Leadership. The purpose of leadership, therefore, is to initiate change for the benefit of society. The civic theme encourages individuals to take action on behalf of the larger common good. Each person has a responsibility to carry change forward.

SOCIAL CHANGE LEADERSHIP INVENTORY

The following statements assess your knowledge and understanding of leadership. Circle the appropriate number (1-5) for each item which best indicates your level of agreement:

1	2	3	4	5
No Knowledge	Little Knowledge	Some Knowledge	Good Knowledge	Substantial Knowledge

1. I recognize the importance leadership plays in groups, organizations, communities, and society.   1   2   3   4   5

2. I recognize that both leaders and followers serve as partners in the leadership and change process.   1   2   3   4   5

3. I understand the relationship between leadership and citizenship. . . .   1   2   3   4   5

4. I am able to recognize, identify, and explain the key concepts, components, and elements of the leadership process.   1   2   3   4   5

5. I understand and recognize the role both personal and collaborative skills play in leadership and the change process.   1   2   3   4   5

6. I am familiar with the concept of "civic leadership" and the pursuit of change for the common (societal) good.   1   2   3   4   5

7. I recognize the key roles of "change, collaboration, and civic responsibility" in the leadership process.   1   2   3   4   5

8. I am able to distinguish between the group stages that lead to coordination, cooperation, and collaboration.   1   2   3   4   5

9. I recognize that every citizen has the ability and obligation to lead.   1   2   3   4   5

10. I am familiar with the concept of "change" and how it is essential to the leadership process.   1   2   3   4   5

11. I recognize the advantages of working in groups to accomplish tasks.   1   2   3   4   5

12. I understand that the primary role of the citizen leader is to address and solve community problems.   1   2   3   4   5

13. I understand that the change process involves challenging the status quo, creating a new vision, and sustaining movement.   1   2   3   4   5

14. I understand that the goal of collaborative leadership is to assist people in working together to solve problems.   1   2   3   4   5

15. I understand that those who participate in civic leadership serve as agents of change to make our world a better place.   1   2   3   4   5

SOCIAL CHANGE LEADERSHIP INVENTORY

The following statements assess the extent to which you engage in leadership actions, behaviors, and activities. Circle the appropriate number (1-5) for each item which best applies to your practice:

1	2	3	4	5
	Once in		Fairly	Almost
Rarely	a While	Sometimes	Often	Always

16. Either as a leader or follower participating in leadership, I am committed to making positive change. 1 2 3 4 5

17. I demonstrate collaborative leadership skills, including the ability to successfully communicate and work with others in group settings. 1 2 3 4 5

18. I serve as a citizen leader in my community. 1 2 3 4 5

19. I actively challenge the way things are done in the groups and organizations in which I participate. 1 2 3 4 5

20. I encourage people to work together and collaborate with one another in a team approach. 1 2 3 4 5

21. I am personally committed to leadership and civic change as a way to serve others. 1 2 3 4 5

22. I actively encourage, promote, and support positive change in the groups and organizations in which I participate. 1 2 3 4 5

23. I treat other team members with dignity and respect. 1 2 3 4 5

24. I volunteer time to serve others in my community. 1 2 3 4 5

25. I work hard to sustain long-term positive change in the groups and organizations in which I participate. 1 2 3 4 5

26. I encourage team members to feel a sense of ownership for the common goals we pursue. 1 2 3 4 5

27. I attend and actively participate in community meetings and forums in order to make a difference. 1 2 3 4 5

28. I see myself as a "change agent" in the groups and organizations in which I participate. 1 2 3 4 5

29. I encourage and support a climate of mutual trust among team members. 1 2 3 4 5

30. I serve as an agent of change for the purpose of making my community and world a better place. 1 2 3 4 5

SCORING YOUR SCL INVENTORY

Your *SCL Inventory* can be scored in three different ways: first, your knowledge and understanding of leadership; second, your commitment and participation in leadership; and third, your total score which reflects both your leadership understanding and behavior. ***The higher your score, the better you understand and participate in the basic principles of social change leadership.***

MY UNDERSTANDING OF LEADERSHIP

Add all your response numbers from statements 1 – 15. . . . .

- ♦ A low score ranges from 15 – 35.
- ♦ A medium score ranges from 36 – 55.
- ♦ A high score ranges from 56 – 75.

This score reflects your general knowledge and understanding of leadership.

MY PRACTICE OF LEADERSHIP BEHAVIOR

Add all your response numbers from statements 16 – 30. . . . .

- ♦ A low score ranges from 15 – 35.
- ♦ A medium score ranges from 36 – 55.
- ♦ A high score ranges from 56 – 75.

This score reflects the extent to which you actually engage in leadership behavior.

TOTAL SCORE: MY UNDERSTANDING AND PRACTICE OF LEADERSHIP

Add your understanding and behavior subscores together to determine
your *SCL Inventory* total score. . . . .

- ♦ A low score ranges from 30 – 70.
- ♦ A medium score ranges from 71 – 110.
- ♦ A high score ranges from 111 – 150.

*This score reflects both your general knowledge of leadership and your commitment
and participation level in social change leadership.*

To learn more about your knowledge and practice of social change leadership, please transfer your scores to pages 16 and 17 of this workbook and follow all instructions

"Civic participation is not an elective but a given."

-Cheryl Mabey

CPSIA information can be obtained at www.ICGtesting.com
Printed in the USA
LVOW02s2032280515

440322LV00002B/2/P